FROM BURNOUT TO BLISS

THE ULTIMATE

90-DAY GUIDE FOR

EMOTIONAL AND MENTAL

ABUNDANCE

DEDICATION

This book is dedicated in memory of my beloved brother John, who would have been celebrating his 57th birthday on the 4th April 2023. Sadly John lost his battle for cancer, only 4 months after being diagnosed. Despite his unwavering determination. John's last words of encouragement, continue to inspire me every day.

"Continue to make me proud, Little Sis. You are going to rock this world" – John May 2022

John, your unwavering support and belief in me will always be cherished. Your passing was a great loss to everyone, who knew you, as you touched our hearts, with you sense of fun, loving nature, passion for life and your love of music, but your memory will live on through the pages of this book. I hope that this book will not only make you proud, but will also help others find their own path to freedom and transformation.

Contents

BIO

"What you think people perceive you as, isn't necessarily what is real."

Keely Woolley

1

MY STORY

Do you remember those parties, the masquerade parties, where you don't know the real person behind the mask? It can be quite exciting and mysterious, can't it? And yet, what if you had to wear that mask all the time?

This is where my journey begins and led to me writing this book.

As I was heading towards security at Schiphol Airport, Amsterdam, in December 2019. I could hear the hustle & bustle and excitement of everyone around me, looking forward to the journey ahead, but I wasn't feeling their excitement. Only the crushing session on my chest, as my breathing go faster, and my thoughts spun around like a carousel in my head, as I replayed the car crash of the interview I had just had for a role in our new organisation.

I was struggling to put one foot in front of the other as I reached the top of the escalator, and my legs buckled from under me. I don't remember much after that, only waking up to see her brown eyes looking down at me, with her dark her bob framing her round face. She's a bit like Dawn French from the Vicar of Dibley, but unlike her, her smile doesn't meet her eyes. Joyce has that look of disappointment and concern, and I don't want to hear what she has to say.

3

"Keely, when are you going to stop focusing on everyone else, putting them first all the time? When are you going to listen to Lauren? You can't take responsibility for everyone. They are all adults."

"But that's the problem Joyce, I do feel responsible, and every time I have to put another member of my team at risk, I feel like I am dying inside"

"I know, Keely, but there is only so much you can do. You need to focus on your own future and well-being. And don't think for a second that smile on your face is fooling, anybody. You are just not coping"

I knew Joyce was right, but despite her advice, I continued to focus on my team, but that was until a month later, when I received the call from H.R. and after over 23 years working within the same company, Joyce tells me, that I was unsuccessful in my interview and was going to be put at risk for redundancy. At that moment, the world collapsed around me, and I mentally and physically shut down completely.

Maybe you've had a time when you have put on a brave face for everyone else around you, to the detriment of your own health.

Over the coming months, I had to make some life-changing decisions about my future, but mentally, I wasn't ready to deal with anything. They signed me off sick. I couldn't talk to my family and friends. Ironically, COVID has struck and I couldn't even talk to my therapist.

So, I had to find a way. I had to do it myself.

I started to RESET, by walking my dogs daily and doing gardening. It turns out I really enjoyed it, which is just as well, as I hadn't touched it in over 20 years. I am not saying it was overgrown, but I had created my own forest.

I then began to RENERGISE through yoga and meditation, and I learnt the importance of gratitude and intention. My sleep started to improve, as I had reduced the amount of technological I was using throughout the day. I started to read and listen to books about burnout, imposter-syndrome and stress management. Find your why by Simon Sinek and Give and Take by Adam Grant.

Slowly, I started to improve, and during my journey of recovery, I began to REFLECT on the past, what went well, what didn't go so well and when did things change. Joyce's, words kept repeating in my head and realised that I had put everyone else first, and not set personal boundaries, always trying to prove myself and volunteering for everything. I feared judgment, feared saying no and feared being seen as weak. What I didn't know was why.

That was until a month later, and I am in my garden. The sun is shining, I have my shorts and t-shirt on. I am laying on the sun lounger with a gin and tonic in one hand and yet another book, in the other hand. "Stop People-Pleasing" by Patrick King. And there was one thing he said, that stood out to me, and it wasn't that people-pleasing was a symptom. I already knew that. It was that you needed to identify the root cause, the origin of why. And one of the key origin reasons he mentioned was the "Fear of Confrontation". Not rocking the boat, keeping the peace, and making everybody happy.

And that was when it hit me. I did want to keep everyone happy and please them all the time. Because when everybody is happy, that's good. But when they are not happy, that's bad. As they become unpredictable and I had to protect myself and protect those around me. Unfortunately, this trait wasn't serving me or anyone around me at all. As I was no longer fully present, I didn't have any energy or spare capacity left and I was being irritable and impatient with the key people in my life. That was what I knew I had to change.

There was one big positive realisation, whilst I was reflecting on the past. I realised that over the last 23 years in a Global Corporate Environment, in my Executive role. I loved coaching, training and mentoring other people, and I was really good at it. Helping them to grow, seeing them transform, and the light shine in their eyes when they have that eureka moment and achieve success.

That's when I realised I needed to step away from the corporate role for good, and do what I loved instead. I had finally woken up, REDISCOVERED my WHY. So, I took the redundancy and decided to set up my own coaching business to help others. Which is when Metamorforsuccess Inspiring Leadership Endeavour, came alive.

Have you ever had that feeling, where the veil is slowly starting to lift and you know there is more to this in life, but you are not quite sure what it is? But what happens if there is a way that someone can shortcut that in life and

help you to lift it off altogether, and discover your true identity? Just imagine how much fulfilment and success you could gain. Wouldn't that be a person worth talking to?

It wasn't always easy, and I would love to tell you that everything was perfect and I had queues of clients knocking on my door overnight.

And my family questioned me about setting up my own coaching business. "Isn't that a big risk, Keely? You have no other income coming into the home."

My friends were saying, "What do you know about running your own coaching business?"

But I knew this was right. I had rediscovered my "why", which was helping others to REDISCOVER their WHY. See the light shine in their eyes, when they have those Eureka moments, and become even more fulfilled and successful in life, personally and professionally.

That's my "WHY."

And little by little, things started to improve. My first small win was helping my husband. And yes, I know the old saying, "Don't work with children and animals", "Or husbands." Well, I did work with mine and helped him to unlock something that was causing him anxiety and transformed his thought process.

Then I helped one of my clients, Lisa, to rediscover her "why" and establish what she really wanted. Which was to have control over her own destiny and well-being, something she had never had. Now she is running her own business and truly doing what she believes in.

And then I did my first 5-day challenge, and in just 24 hours, I helped Sammie to realise that she could be vulnerable and open with her family and team. She didn't need to work a 70-hour week, and was hiding from a problem she didn't want to face. Subsequently, she is working fewer hours, her relationships, sleep and her physical and mental health have improved, and company performance has increased.

And now I get to help my clients, using my Freedom Transformation Formula, inspiring them to REDISCOVER their WHY and Bounceback from burnout, without compromising their dreams or career.

Which I would like to share with you. But before I continue, let me leave you with this thought.

Sometimes you might feel like you are wearing that masquerade mask, but when you finally take it off, it's like discovering a hidden purpose; a freeing feeling of being able to pursue what you love and find joy in.

INTRODUCTION

"You may have a purpose, but unless you are willing to take that leap of faith and take a risk, you will never get the opportunity to live your purpose"

Keely Woolley

Maybe the vision you had in mind for yourself, is not being realised in the way you hoped anymore and you are feeling frustrated and demotivated, which means that you are finding your sleep is beginning to deteriorate and you are feeling increasingly anxious.

Possibly you are becoming busier and busier in life, and have no time to resolve the problems that need resolving, and you question your next move. Which means that you are taking calls at evenings and weekends, saying those inevitable words, just 5 minutes, just 5 minutes, and we all know it's more time spent without family or friends, and life is passing you by.

Perhaps, you are feeling like an imposter, and you wonder how you got into the role you are in, and you wonder when you will get found out. So, you are always trying to prove yourself and volunteering for everything, which means that you are becoming exhausted and burnout.

Potentially, you are feeling like every single day is like ground-hog day, and you've hit that concrete ceiling and you wonder what the future has in mind for you, but you know it's not this. Which means that you are becoming increasingly less tolerant with the key people in your life and it's affecting your relationships, personally and professionally.

Imagine, it's 6 a.m in the morning, and you turn to your alarm clock and you find you have another 30 mins before the alarm goes off, but you don't mind, because you are sleeping like a baby, and loving and living your life with passion and purpose.

Picture, a time when the key people in your life, are all striving towards a common vision and your values and beliefs are all aligned and you are achieving consistency, in all that you do. Which means that you are finally loving what you are doing, as you have either transformed within the business your are in or created a new one.

Visualise, a future where you feel empowered and motivated, within the organisation you are in, and you are seen as an inspiration leader, where others are knocking down your door, to either come and work with them or for you, because people are loving the culture and environment that you have created.

Envisage, that time where you finally have that freedom, and you get to spend time with family and friends, or time alone, because no-one is disturbing your piece.

If you, want to take control of your life, so that you can have a more balanced, fulfilling and successful life, whilst becoming even healthier mentally and physically? Then the "Freedom Transformation Formula®" might be the solution for you.

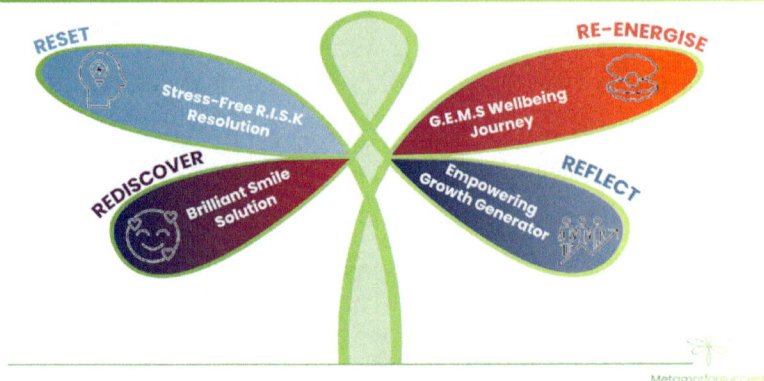

Diagram 1 – Freedom Transformation Formula®

In this book we will explore the first stage of the Freedom Transformation Formula®, which is **RESET**. And what does that mean? It's about being able to reset where you are now mentally and physically, and being able to reset what you're doing, and begin the healing process to start reducing the amount of stress, anxiety, and burnout in your life.

You will discover tools, techniques and strategies to enable you to RESET and recognise your key driver for stress.

At the same time, establish why is it so important to reset and recognise your stress! As, without recognising your stress, the hidden effects of stress and anxiety can be hugely damaging to both your mental and physical health. If it's not removed, you may experience sleepless nights, brain fog, headaches, memory loss, and other negative impacts on your health. It can also lead to self-sabotage, such as drinking too much alcohol, eating unhealthy foods, not exercising, and neglecting self-care.

You will learn how The Stress-free R.I.S.K Resolution® framework provides you step-by-step guidance to break the patterns of burnout and become empowered to build a mindset of peace and purpose.

By using the Stress-free R.I.S.K Resolution® framework, you can identify your key drivers for stress and create an awareness of your indicators for stress. This will allow you to address your stress head-on, rather than letting it continue to cause damage to your mental and physical health. The framework provides concrete strategies for reducing stress, anxiety, and burnout, as well as tools for improving overall well-being and taking control of one's life.

You will learn the importance of Practicing Self-Love and Self-Awareness. Throughout the process of resetting and managing stress, we encourage you to practice self-love and self-awareness so that you can achieve lasting, positive change. By prioritising self-care, setting boundaries, and making sustainable changes, readers can create a foundation for long-term stress management and improved well-being.

You will learn the foundation for growth and transformation

By resetting and taking action to manage stress, you can begin to live a more balanced and fulfilling life. The RESET stage is the foundation for the rest of the Freedom Transformation Formula® and sets the stage for growth and transformation. So, if you're ready to take control of your life, reduce your stress and anxiety, and achieve lasting, positive change, the "Freedom Transformation Formula" may be the perfect solution for you

CHAPTER 1 - BELIEFS AND BURNOUT: THE LINK BETWEEN YOUR THOUGHTS AND YOUR STRESS LEVELS

"Self-care is not selfish. You cannot serve from an empty vessel."

Eleanor Brown

Burnout and stress are often self-driven patterns of behaviour caused by an individual's own thoughts, beliefs, and actions. Unfortunately, many female executives, leaders, founders & entrepreneurs don't recognise the signs of burnout and stress or take the necessary steps to manage and prevent it. This is where the Stress-free R.I.S.K Resolution framework comes in. By recognising your key drivers for stress and creating awareness of your indicators for stress, and addressing your stress, you can start to improve your overall well-being and take control of your life through self-love and self-awareness.

Creating and setting boundaries between your personal and business life is an essential part of managing stress and burnout. Setting boundaries helps ensure that work-related responsibilities do not overwhelm you and can focus on the tasks that are most important and will help you be more productive. However, many female executives, leaders, founder & entrepreneurs make the mistake of thinking they don't have time to set boundaries, which can lead to overworking and burnout. By setting a specific time to begin and end work each day and limiting the amount of time spent on each task, you can avoid overworking and achieve a better work-life balance.

Making time for yourself is also essential for managing stress and burnout. It allows you to reset, re-energise, and refocus, increasing your performance personally and professionally. However, many females believe they are coping with life and feel they have to soldier on, regardless. Scheduling time-out for yourself throughout the day to relax your mind and recharge is essential for managing stress and burnout.

Prioritising self-care is another important principle. When you practise self-care, it helps ensure you are physically and mentally healthy, improving your overall well-being and allowing you to perform at your best. Many female executives, leaders and founders make the mistake of thinking that self-care is not important, but it is crucial for managing stress and burnout.

The key to a stress-free life is to recognise your key drivers and indicators for stress and establishing your patterns of behaviour. That way, you'll be able to develop strategies to avoid or manage stress in your life, avoid increasing your stress levels, and avoid impacting your relationships and productivity. By using the Stress-free R.I.S.K Resolution framework, you'll be able to achieve a more fulfilled and successful life, personally and professionally, without needing to be superhuman, perfect, or like someone you're not.

So, here's the KEY! The KEY to a stress-free life is by recognising your key drivers and indicators for stress and establishing your patterns of behaviour. That way, you'll be able to develop strategies to avoid or manage stress in your life without affecting your relationships or productivity. Even if you fear judgment, think taking time for yourself is selfish, feel overwhelmed by your current situation, or feel you don't have the knowledge or tools to make changes, this book will guide you step-by-step to achieve a stress-free life.

Throughout this book, I will explain WHY almost everything you've been trying to do to BounceBack from Burnout is NOW going to make things HARDER. But also, explain why almost everything you're doing to solve BounceBack from Burnout is unnecessary and a waste of your valuable time. With the Stress-free R.I.S.K Resolution framework, you'll be able to learn how to bounce back from burnout and manage stress in your life effectively, without needing to be superhuman or perfect.

This book provides you with solutions and strategies to resolve the problems identified by readers originally, ensuring you achieve it through self-love and self-awareness. So, get ready to transform your life and achieve your goals with the Stress-free R.I.S.K Resolution framework.

NOW, the reason why things may become harder is that the Stress-free R.I.S.K Resolution framework requires you to look within and challenge your own thoughts and beliefs, which can be uncomfortable and difficult at times. However, it is only by identifying and addressing these underlying patterns of behaviour that you can achieve positive and sustainable results in managing stress and preventing burnout.

By doing the hard work of introspection and self-reflection, you will be able to recognise your key drivers and indicators for stress, establish your patterns of behaviour, and develop strategies to avoid or manage stress in your life. This process requires a willingness to be honest with yourself and make changes that may challenge your current way of thinking and living.

But ultimately, by investing in yourself and taking the necessary steps to manage your stress and prevent burnout, you will be able to lead a more fulfilled and successful life, personally and professionally. The key is to approach the process with a positive mindset and a willingness to do the hard work, knowing that the rewards will be worth the effort.

In conclusion, burnout and stress can be caused by an individual's own thoughts, beliefs, and actions. Unfortunately, many people don't recognise the signs of burnout and stress or take the necessary steps to manage and prevent it. The Stress-free R.I.S.K Resolution framework helps individuals recognise their key drivers for stress and develop strategies to avoid or manage stress in their lives, through self-love and self-awareness. Creating boundaries, making time for oneself, and prioritising self-care are all essential parts of managing stress and preventing burnout. By recognising and establishing patterns of behaviour, individuals can develop strategies to avoid or manage stress in their lives and achieve a more fulfilled and successful life, both personally and professionally. The Stress-free R.I.S.K Resolution framework requires individuals to look within and challenge their own thoughts and beliefs, which can be uncomfortable and difficult at times. But by investing in oneself and taking the necessary steps to manage stress and prevent burnout, individuals can lead a more fulfilled and successful life, knowing that the rewards will be worth the effort.

CHAPTER 2: THE ROAD MAP TO RELAXATION: RECOGNISE YOUR KEY DRIVERS FOR STRESS

"It's not stress that kills us, it is our reaction to it."

Hans Selye

In this chapter, we explore the journey towards relaxation and how we can identify and **RECOGNISE** the key drivers of stress in our lives. We'll look at the different types of stress and how they manifest in our bodies and minds. We'll also examine the importance of monitoring and tracking our stress levels throughout the day and explore the different tools and techniques we can use to do this effectively. Finally, we'll look at the importance of understanding our reactions to stress and developing strategies to help us respond differently and take control of our lives.

We will also explore the Relaxing Road M.A.P.S system, which involves four key Steps to establish how to RECOGNISE our key driver for stress and the management of stress and begin the recuperation process and become even more stress-free and relaxed. Which is achieved by taking control of our emotional responses and using our logical brain to develop new strategies. So that we can show up as true leaders both personally and professionally.

We share how the Relaxing Road M.A.P.S system is associated to the principles of the Neuro Linguistic Programming (NLP) communication model in relation to our six senses, and the fight, flight, and freeze response of our emotional monkey brain. And how they can be used to reframe our thinking, language, and how to respond to situations in a more positive and productive way.

The first key step in the Stress-Free R.I.S.K Resolution is **RECOGNITION**. Which means being able to recognise your key drivers for stress and how stress exhibits itself. It's essential to understand that stress can occur for different reasons, and the levels in which stress can increase depend on the circumstances associated with it.

It's also important to note that there is a difference between good stress and bad stress. Good stress can motivate and push us to achieve our goals and can even be necessary for growth and development. Examples of good stress include starting a new job or taking on a new challenge. However, bad stress can have a serious impact on our health, both mentally and physically.

When we experience bad stress, our bodies release cortisol and other stress hormones, which can lead to long-term damage to our physical and mental health. Examples of bad stress include experiencing a traumatic event, facing financial difficulties, or experiencing ongoing conflict in relationships.

At the end of this chapter, I share a link to the free Daily Stress Monitor Tracker, which I share with my clients to start monitoring their stress levels throughout the day and during their 12 week programme. This tool helps my clients build a picture of their current situation and their progress over time. I invite you to download this free tracker to monitor your own progress.

The measurement ranges from a level of zero to 10, with zero being good and 10 being very stressed. This should be used to record good days or bad days and capture what made the day good or stressful, including events, people, places, and activities. This helps to recognise and understand the key drivers and triggers with regards to the levels of stress.

By building a pattern and recognising the tell-tale signs of stress from the outset, you can start understanding your patterns of behaviour. One of the biggest mistakes people make is not recognising their key drivers and patterns of behaviour, which leads to a self-perpetuating cycle of stress and anxiety. When it becomes chronic, it can become too late to do anything about it, leading to full burnout.

It is important to note external factors will always impact us in life, and we rarely have control over the situation. However, when we understand the key drivers for stress, we can put mechanisms in place to mitigate or eliminate the impact of events. Unfortunately, when people don't understand their key drivers for stress, they can behave in a less than pleasing manner as their emotional monkey kicks in, and they react in an uncontrolled way, rather than applying our "logical brain".

When I mention the "emotional monkey" versus the "logical brain," I am referring to the two parts of our brain that are responsible for decision making. The emotional monkey is the amygdala, which is responsible for processing emotions and initiating the fight-or-flight response. The logical brain is the prefrontal cortex, which is responsible for reasoning, planning, and decision making.

When we are experiencing stress, our emotional monkey can take over and cause us to make impulsive decisions based on our emotions rather than logic. This can lead to irrational behaviour and poor decision making. On the other hand, when we engage our logical brain, we are able to think through a situation, weigh the pros and cons, and make a decision based on rational thought.

It's important to recognise when our emotional monkey is taking over and try to engage our logical brain in decision making. You can be achieve this by taking a step back, taking deep breaths, and giving yourself time to process your emotions before making a decision. It can also be helpful to write down your thoughts and feelings to gain clarity and perspective on the situation. By engaging our logical brain, we can make better decisions that are in line with our goals and values.

"The Tortoise and the Hare" is a great example as to how our emotional monkey brain can have an impact on our performance. The hare is so focused on winning the race that he burns himself out and loses in the end. The tortoise, on the other hand, takes a slower and steadier approach and ends up winning. This story illustrates the importance of monitoring your pace and not letting stress and the pressure, get the best of you.

In the next chapter, I will share how you can establish your key drivers for stress by following the 4 key steps of the Relaxing Road M.A.P.S System.

Case Study:

Let me introduce one of my clients, Sammie Engleby. When I first started working with her, she initially said that she wanted to learn tools and techniques for stress management with her own team in her business. Sammie didn't even realise that she was stressed, despite working a 70-hour week.

During our group sessions, she soon described herself as an individual, that in certain situations, she would go from 0 to def con 9 in 60 seconds. Become emotional, shoot from the hip and react in a way that wasn't her usual self. Ironically, Sammie wasn't even aware she was doing this, until she started to monitor and track her stress levels and response to those situations.

And yet, when Sammie realised what she was doing, and that she was allowing her "Emotional Monkey" to takeover, during challenging times and events. Sammie started to take a moment to breathe and reflect on the situation and refocus. Which means that, her logical brain is given a chance to engage and respond in a constructive manner.

Sammie also realised that she wasn't allowing any time for herself throughout the day to **RESET**. She remained at her desk all day, with no breaks at all. Which subsequently increased her stress levels, further. Sammie, has now scheduled in her diary, a 5 minute break, every hour to take time out and walk away from her desk and take a breather. Obviously, only when it was a convenient moment, of course. Even now, when Sammie and I speak, she tells me how she still keeps her "Emotional Monkey" firmly under control. Which makes me smile.

Sammie had other key learnings, and we will tap into them throughout this book.

In conclusion, this chapter delves into the importance of recognising and identifying the key drivers of stress in our lives. We learned about the different types of stress and how they manifest in our bodies and minds, as well as the significance of monitoring and tracking our stress levels throughout the day. By using tools and techniques like the Daily Stress Monitor Tracker and following the four key steps of the Relaxing Road M.A.P.S System, we can understand our patterns of behaviour and develop new strategies to respond to stress and take control of our lives. We also learned about the two parts of our brain responsible for decision-making - the emotional monkey and the logical brain - and the importance of engaging our logical brain to make better decisions. By following these steps, we can all develop greater awareness and control over our stress levels, become more resilient, and show up as leaders both personally and professionally.

Click on the QR Code for a Free
Daily Stress Monitor - Tracker

QR Code to Daily Stress Monitor – Tracker

CHAPTER 3: NAVIGATING THE RELAXING ROAD: 4 KEY STEPS TO RECOGNISE AND MANAGE STRESS DRIVERS

"Tension is who you think you should be. Relaxation is who you are."

Chinese proverb

In this chapter, we'll dive deeper into the Relaxing Road M.A.P.S® system introduced in Chapter 2 and explore the four key Steps you can take to monitor and manage your stress levels:

By following the Relaxing Road M.A.P.S® system and taking these four key Steps, you can build greater awareness and control over your stress levels, develop resilience and a proactive mindset, and show up as a leader that others will follow, whether that is personally or professionally.

Step 1 - Monitor and Track Your Stress Levels: The first key step that is required to recognise the key drivers for stress is the importance of monitoring and tracking your daily stress levels. It is important to note, that when we link this to our six senses - sight, sound, taste, smell, touch, and intuition - to identify triggers and patterns of behaviour that lead to stress, it helps us to understand ourselves on a deeper level.

This Step is all about becoming more aware of the stressors in our lives and how they affect us on a daily basis. It's important to notice and become aware of your changing stress levels throughout the day and notice any patterns or triggers that arise. This way, we can start to understand what causes our stress and take action to minimise it.

Think of stress like a car engine. Just as you need to keep track of your car's oil levels and maintenance needs to prevent the engine from breaking down, you also need to monitor your stress levels and take care of your mental and emotional health to prevent burnout.

Step 2 - <u>Ask</u> Exploratory Questions: The next key step is about asking exploratory questions and getting curious about our feelings and experiences in relation to specific events and situations that may increase stress levels. When I have worked with my clients using the questionnaire, which I share with you at the bottom of this chapter, it helps them to get a deeper understanding of themselves and their triggers better in specific situations that may have caused them stress in the past or throughout this process.

By understanding the context of these situations, you can better understand your own behaviour and reactions. This is where the emotional monkey brain comes in, as it can trigger the fight, flight, or freeze response.

Think of stress like an onion. The outer layers are the visible symptoms, but by peeling back the layers and asking exploratory questions, we can get to the root of the problem and find solutions.

By recognising these reactions and using our logical brain to take a breath, think, and refocus, we can regain control of the situation. It is important to note that I use the word reaction, rather than respond, as being reactive means we are not in control of the situation. We will take a deep-dive into this area further on.

In the movie "The Lion King," Simba experiences a lot of stress and anxiety after the death of his father. It's only when he starts asking questions and exploring his feelings with Rafiki that he begins to understand himself better and gain the confidence to take action.

31

Step 3 - Establish **Patterns** of Behaviour: Once we have identified our key drivers and triggers for stress, we can explore and examine our reactions to different situations, and how they impact our patterns of behaviour or habits that may be causing us harm or potentially those around us. By doing so, you can develop a greater awareness of your own behaviour and start to break free from them and make more informed decisions and establish healthier habits about how to respond to stress.

Think of stress like a river. If we keep reacting to the same stressors in the same way, we'll keep getting swept downstream. But by establishing new patterns of behaviour, we can create eddies and currents that allow us to navigate the river more effectively.

Step 4 - Identify **Strategies** and Take Control: With this final step, we can now consider specific strategies and techniques for responding to stress and taking control of the situation. By exploring how you can develop a more proactive mindset, identify solutions to problems and develop a plan of action, you can feel more confident and in control, and take actions that align with your values and goals. With practice, these strategies can help build resilience and to show up as a true leader in both your personal and professional life.

In conclusion, managing stress effectively requires a proactive approach that involves monitoring and tracking our stress levels, asking exploratory questions, establishing new patterns of behavior, and identifying strategies to take control. By following the Relaxing Road M.A.P.S system and these four key steps, we can develop greater awareness and control over our stress levels, build resilience, and show up as leaders in our personal and professional lives. We need to recognize that stress is a part of life, but it is how we respond to it that makes the difference. By taking a proactive approach, we can gain a deeper understanding of ourselves, our triggers, and how to manage our stress levels. This will not only improve our mental and emotional health but also help us to build better relationships with others and achieve our goals. Remember, stress is like a river, and we need to learn how to navigate it effectively to reach our destination. With practice and dedication, we can develop the skills and strategies to do just that.

Click on the QR Code for a Free
Recognising Key Drivers for Stress

Scan QR Code - Recognising Key Drivers for Stress

CHAPTER 4: MASTERING STRESS: RESPONDING VS. REACTING FOR GREATER CONTROL AND WELL-BEING

"Stress is not what happens to us. It's our response to what happens. And response is something we can choose."

Maureen Killoran

One strategy I mentioned previously was the importance of responding to situations, rather than reacting. Here's why.

Responding to situations instead of reacting is a crucial aspect of managing stress and maintaining control in our lives. Reacting to situations often involves an emotional response, where we act impulsively without much thought, driven by our emotional monkey, and without much control over the situation. In contrast, responding involves a more logical approach where we take a step back, assess the situation, and choose our response carefully. When we respond to situations, we are taking control of the situation rather than letting it control us.

It's important to understand that how we react or respond to situations can have a significant impact on ourselves and those around us. For instance, when we react destructively, it can create tension and conflict with others, making the situation worse. Moreover, it can also impact our own mental and physical health. In contrast, responding constructively can help resolve conflicts, improve relationships, and even reduce stress levels.

When we react, we are often perceived, as being out of control, emotional, reactive, and unpredictable. However, when we respond constructively, we are seen as being in control, thoughtful, and rational. This can help us to earn respect from others, and establish ourselves as reliable, trustworthy and competent.

Being able to respond instead of reacting requires practice, and it's not always easy, especially when we are under stress or pressure. It's important to be aware of our emotional monkey and to take steps to manage our emotions so that we can respond constructively to situations. This might include techniques such as taking a deep breath, counting to ten, or taking a break to reflect on the situation.

Overall, the ability to respond constructively rather than reactively can make a significant difference in our lives, enabling us to maintain control, manage stress, and build positive relationships with others.

As mentioned earlier, it's important to recognise that we can't control external factors in our lives, such as the behaviour of others. For example, we may have a colleague or team member who interrupts us, doesn't listen to our ideas, or takes credit for our work. This behaviour can be frustrating and even harmful to our work and well-being.

However, it's important to remember that we do have control over how we respond to these situations. Reacting impulsively, emotionally or with anger can lead to negative outcomes, such as damaging relationships or losing respect from others. Instead, it's better to respond thoughtfully and constructively.

One way to do this is by showing compassion and gratitude towards the individual who may have taken credit for your work or idea. Rather than reacting defensively or aggressively, try acknowledging their input and contribution to the idea while also asserting that it was originally your idea. This can help diffuse tension and show that you are a strong and confident leader who is willing to share credit.

By responding in a calm and respectful manner, you are also taking control of the situation and showing that you won't be thrown off course by external factors. This approach can also help you to build better relationships with your colleagues and team members, leading to a more positive and productive work environment.

Overall, it's important to remember that we can't control external factors in our lives, but we can control how we respond to them. By responding thoughtfully and constructively, we can create a more positive impact on ourselves and those around us.

Think of stress like a battlefield. If we go in unprepared and without a plan, we're likely to get overwhelmed and defeated. But by identifying our strategies and taking control, we can approach each stressor with a clear plan of action.

In conclusion, responding instead of reacting is an essential strategy for managing stress and maintaining control in our lives. When we respond constructively, we take control of the situation and choose our response thoughtfully, rather than being controlled by our emotions. By doing so, we can create a positive impact on ourselves and those around us, improve our relationships, and reduce stress levels. Remember that we can't always control external factors, but we can control our response to them. By being prepared, identifying our strategies, and taking control, we can approach each stressor with a clear plan of action. With practice, we can develop the ability to respond constructively to situations and lead a more balanced and fulfilling life.

CHAPTER 5: MASTERING EMOTIONAL INTELLIGENCE: THE KEY TO EFFECTIVE STRESS MANAGEMENT

"Emotional intelligence is the ability to recognise our own feelings and those of others, and to manage emotions effectively in ourselves and our relationships."

Daniel Goleman

Building upon the previous chapter, managing stress effectively requires a high level of emotional intelligence. Emotional intelligence is the ability to identify and manage one's own emotions and those of others. It involves being aware of one's emotional state and using that awareness to make effective decisions and communicate effectively.

In the context of stress management, emotional intelligence can help individuals identify the emotions that are driving their stress and take steps to manage those emotions effectively. For example, someone who is experiencing high levels of stress due to a difficult work situation may be feeling frustrated, overwhelmed, and anxious. By identifying and acknowledging these emotions, the individual can take steps to manage them, such as by taking a break, practicing mindfulness, or seeking support from a colleague or manager.

Emotional intelligence also involves being able to communicate effectively with others, which can be important in managing stress in the workplace. As mentioned in the previous chapter, when someone who is experiencing stress due to a difficult colleague or manager may need to communicate their concerns and needs in a clear and assertive way. By doing so, they can work towards resolving the situation and reducing their stress levels.

Overall, emotional intelligence plays a critical role in managing stress effectively. By developing emotional intelligence skills such as self-awareness, self-regulation, and effective communication, individuals can take control of their emotions and create a more balanced and fulfilling life.

In conclusion, emotional intelligence is a key component of effective stress management. It involves being aware of one's own emotions and those of others, and using that awareness to make effective decisions and communicate effectively. By developing emotional intelligence skills such as self-awareness, self-regulation, and effective communication, individuals can take control of their emotions and manage stress effectively. By identifying the emotions driving their stress, individuals can take steps to manage those emotions effectively, and communicate their needs and concerns in a clear and assertive way. Ultimately, developing emotional intelligence can help individuals create a more balanced and fulfilling life, free from the negative impacts of stress.

CHAPTER 6: BREAKING FREE FROM THE CYCLE OF PEOPLE-PLEASING: UNDERSTANDING THE CONNECTIONS & ROOT-CAUSE

"If you live for people's acceptance, you'll die from their rejection."

Lecrae

As I mentioned earlier, burnout and stress can often be self-driven patterns of behaviour caused by an individual's own thoughts, beliefs, and actions. For me, one of those patterns of behaviour was people-pleasing. I felt like I needed to say yes to every request, every favour, every demand placed on me by others. I thought that by doing so, I would be seen as helpful, reliable, and dependable. But what I didn't realise was that my people-pleasing tendencies were taking a toll on my mental and physical health.

When you're constantly saying yes to others, you're inevitably saying no to yourself. You're putting everyone else's needs and wants above your own, and in doing so, you're neglecting your own self-care. This can lead to feelings of resentment, exhaustion, and burnout. And yet, it can be hard to break free from the cycle of people-pleasing, especially if you've been doing it for years. But here's the thing: being a people-pleaser isn't sustainable. It's not a healthy way to live, and it's not a path to long-term happiness and fulfilment. In fact, it's quite the opposite. People-pleasing can lead to anxiety, depression, and a whole host of physical health problems.

That's why it's so important to prioritise your own needs and wants, even if it means saying no to others. It's not selfish to take care of yourself; in fact, it's essential. Furthermore, you are being selfish to yourself, when you don't learn to say no to others. When you're feeling your best, you're able to show up for others in a more meaningful and impactful way. And when you're able to set healthy boundaries and prioritise your own well-being, you'll find that you're more productive, more creative, and more fulfilled than ever before.

As we have discussed, people-pleasing can have a detrimental impact on your mental and physical health, leading to burnout and stress. But it's important to understand that people-pleasing is not the problem in and of itself; it's merely a symptom of a deeper issue.

To truly overcome people-pleasing and prevent burnout, it's crucial to identify the origins, or root cause, of this behaviour. This may involve exploring past experiences or traumas that have led you to believe that pleasing others is necessary for your own survival or success. By identifying these origins, you can develop a more comprehensive plan for overcoming people-pleasing and building a healthier, more fulfilling life.

In conclusion, the cycle of people-pleasing can have a serious impact on your well-being and lead to burnout and stress. While it may be challenging to break free from this pattern of behaviour, it's important to prioritise your own needs and wants, even if it means saying no to others. This is not selfish, but rather essential for your own self-care and long-term happiness.

It's important to understand that people-pleasing is merely a symptom of a deeper issue, and identifying the root cause of this behaviour is crucial for overcoming it. This may involve exploring past experiences or traumas that have led you to believe that pleasing others is necessary for your own survival or success. With a comprehensive plan for addressing the root cause of people-pleasing, you can build a healthier, more fulfilling life that allows you to show up for others in a more meaningful way while taking care of yourself. Remember, saying no to others is not a sign of weakness but a sign of strength and self-respect.

CHAPTER 7: THE RELATIONSHIP OF THE RELAXING ROAD M.A.P.S® SYSTEM WITH THE NLP COMMUNICATION MODEL

"The mind is everything. What you think you become."

Buddha

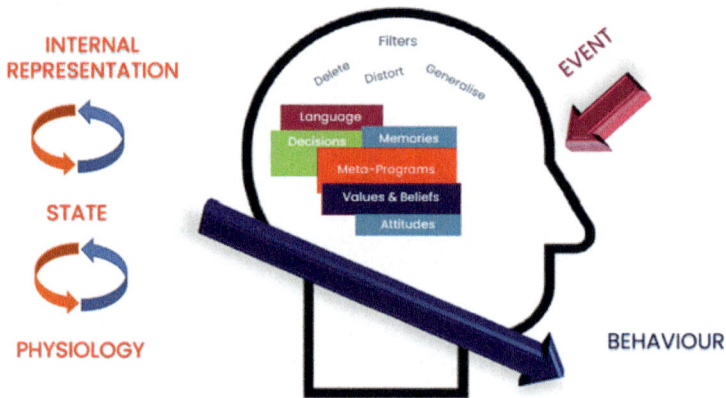

Diagram 2 – Neuro Linguistic Programming (NLP)
Communication Model

The NLP Communication Model is a way of understanding how we process information and experiences through our senses. It involves six senses: sound, sight, touch, smell, taste and internal feelings. In the NLP world, these would be referred to as, visual, auditory, kinaesthetic, olfactory, gustatory, and finally Auditory Digital Each sense is associated with a different type of mental representation or "internal representation" that affects how we experience the world around us.

In relation to the Relaxing Road M.A.P.S® system, the NLP communication model can help us become more aware of how we are processing and experiencing stress in our lives. By monitoring and tracking our daily stress levels and paying attention to the sensory experiences associated with each stressful situation, we can begin to identify our patterns of behaviour and emotional responses that may be contributing to our stress.

As we ask exploratory questions to get a deeper dive into specific situations where we have felt stress, we can use the NLP communication model to identify the sensory experiences associated with each situation. This can help us understand ourselves better and become more aware of how we are processing and experiencing stress.

Once we have established patterns of behaviour and emotional responses to each situation, we can use the NLP communication model to identify strategies for responding differently to each situation. For example, we may learn to focus on a particular sensory experience, such as the feeling of the sun on our skin or the sound of birds chirping, to help us relax and refocus.

In addition, the NLP communication model can help us keep our "emotional monkey" in check by reminding us to stop, take a breath, give ourselves thinking-time, and refocus using our logical brain. By becoming more aware of our sensory experiences and using strategies that work for us, we can take control of our stress and show up as true leaders both personally and professionally.

In the classic fairy tale "Goldilocks and the Three Bears," Goldilocks tries out different chairs, beds, and bowls of porridge until she finds the ones that are "just right." This story illustrates the importance of experimenting with different patterns of behaviour until we find the ones that work best for us.

In conclusion, the NLP communication model can be a powerful tool for identifying patterns of behaviour, emotional responses, and sensory experiences associated with stress. By experimenting with different patterns of behaviour and using strategies that work for us, we can find ways to relax and refocus when stress arises. The NLP communication model reminds us to stop, take a breath, give ourselves thinking-time, and refocus using our logical brain. This way, we can keep our "emotional monkey" in check and take control of our stress levels. By using this tool in conjunction with the Relaxing Road M.A.P.S® system, we can develop strategies for managing stress and become more effective leaders both personally and professionally.

CHAPTER 8: PUTTING YOUR OXYGEN MASK ON FIRST: UNDERSTANDING YOUR KEY INDICATORS FOR STRESS

"The first step towards change is awareness."

Nathaniel Branden

In this chapter, we delve deeper into the key INDICATORS of stress and the importance of being aware of them. Understanding our key indicators for stress is crucial to preventing it from becoming chronic and taking control of our mental and physical health. This next step in the Stress-Free R.I.S.K Resolution® framework is to establish these key indicators and how they display themselves. This can include emotional symptoms like anxiety, as well as physical symptoms like sleepless nights, tiredness, inflamed and aching joints, rashes, weight changes, brain fog, self-sabotage, and changes in eating and drinking patterns.

Monitoring changes in our behaviour, well-being, and physical and mental health over time can help us establish patterns and take steps to protect ourselves. For example, pushing through stress and anxiety without noticing the signals can lead to discombobulation. Essentially, our head and heart are not aligned, causing us to miss the tell-tale signs of burnout.

By monitoring when and what symptoms occur, how long they last, and their frequency, we can prevent stress from becoming chronic and crashing. This is especially important for those with strong personalities who may push through stress without realising its impact on their health.

One example of this is Sammie, who didn't take time out for herself and began reacting to situations in a way that didn't match her normal behaviour. By understanding and monitoring her key indicators for stress, she was able to take steps to prevent herself from reacting impulsively or emotionally in challenging situations.

I often used the analogy of putting on your oxygen mask on first in the context of self-care and stress management. Just as in an emergency on an airplane, where you're instructed to put your own oxygen mask on first before assisting others, the same principle applies to managing stress.

It's important to take care of ourselves first, to ensure that we are in the best position to take care of others. If we neglect our own well-being, we risk becoming overwhelmed and burnt out, which can lead to negative impacts on our physical, emotional, and mental health.

In the context of the Stress-Free R.I.S.K Resolution® framework, recognising and monitoring our key indicators for stress is a key component of putting our own oxygen mask on first. By prioritising our own self-care, we can prevent burnout and be more present and effective for the people we care about.

By taking care of ourselves first, we also set an example for others to follow. We demonstrate that self-care is important and necessary, and we create a positive ripple effect that can benefit not just ourselves, but those around us as well.

Ultimately, the message is clear: taking care of ourselves is not selfish, it's necessary. It's like putting on our own oxygen mask first before assisting others, and it's the best way to ensure that we have the strength and energy to be there for the people we care about most.

In the next chapter, I will share how you can create an awareness of your key indicators for stress by following the 4 key steps of the Powerful A.I.M.S Principle®.

In conclusion, understanding and monitoring our key indicators for stress is essential to preventing chronic stress and taking control of our mental and physical health. By monitoring changes in our behavior, well-being, and physical and mental health over time, we can establish patterns and take steps to protect ourselves. Putting our own oxygen mask on first, prioritizing our own self-care, is necessary to prevent burnout and be more present and effective for the people we care about. It is not selfish, but rather the best way to ensure that we have the strength and energy to be there for others. In the next chapter, the Powerful A.I.M.S Principle® will be introduced as a way to create awareness of our key indicators for stress.

CHAPTER 9: FOLLOW THE POWERFUL A.I.M.S PRINCIPLE®: 4 KEY STEPS FOR CREATING AWARENESS OF YOUR KEY INDICATORS FOR STRESS

"Once we accept our limits, we go beyond them."

Albert Einstein

Step 1: Awareness

It's important to create **AWARENESS** of the key indicators of stress because it helps us recognise when we are feeling stressed and take steps to manage it in the immediate moment and put preventions in place to mitigate or escape it altogether. Research has shown that mindfulness and self-awareness practices can improve our ability to recognise and manage stress.

It's a common belief among many female executives and leaders, that admitting to feeling stressed is a sign of weakness. However, this couldn't be further from the truth. When harnessed in the right way, stress can actually improve focus, increase energy and awareness, and help drive individuals to meet certain challenges. In fact, in emergency situations, stress can even save lives - not just yours, but others' as well. For example, mothers are known to suddenly develop superpowers to save their children or exhibit acute awareness and response in dangerous situations, such as avoiding accidents.

And yet, the problem with ignoring the signs of stress is that it may be too late to reverse the consequences, which can be catastrophic. I am an example of someone who has ignored these signs in the past, and kept focusing on everyone else around me and being their rock, not realising the pains in my neck, shoulder, and arm or becoming less patient with those around me, until I finally crashed altogether. While I did come out the other side, I learned from those experiences and I now coaching and teaching others how to move away from or escape these situations altogether.

There are those who may say that my redundancy was the reason for me crashing, but ultimately, that was the final nail in the coffin. The straw that broke the camel's back.

It's important to monitor any indications and symptoms of stress, such as neck or back pain, changes in eating habits, headaches, and how you respond to those around you. This needs to be done in conjunction with identifying stressful situations.

It's worth noting that what causes stress and symptoms for one person may be different for others. Some of us may experience self-generated internal factors due to our own beliefs or patterns programmed into us, not just external factors.

By monitoring these indicators and symptoms, patterns will start to emerge, increasing personal awareness. This will help individuals find methods to manage and mitigate these situations constructively. In some cases, individuals can even use stress to their advantage to increase personal focus and awareness. Remember, self-care and monitoring your own well-being is not a sign of weakness, but rather a sign of strength and resilience.

In order to create an awareness of your stress levels, it's important to listen to your body and feelings. When you start feeling stressed, take note of how your body is reacting. This can include changes in breathing, heart rate, muscle tension, and energy levels. By observing these changes, you can identify when you are feeling stressed and take action to manage it.

It's also important to identify the key indicators of stress and their impact on your body and mind. This can include physical symptoms like headaches, stomach-aches, and muscle tension, as well as emotional symptoms like irritability, mood swings, and feelings of overwhelm. When you understand how stress affects you personally, you can take steps to manage it more effectively.

Mindfulness techniques such as meditation, deep breathing, and body scanning, can also be helpful in increasing your awareness of your internal state. By practicing these techniques regularly, you can learn to recognise the physical and emotional sensations associated with stress more quickly and effectively, and take steps to manage them before they become overwhelming.

Body scanning is a mindfulness technique that involves focusing your attention on different parts of your body, one at a time, and bringing a non-judgmental awareness to any sensations, tension, or discomfort you may be feeling. This technique helps you to become more aware of the physical sensations in your body, and can help you to release tension and stress in specific areas. By focusing your attention on your body, you are also bringing your mind to the present moment, which is a key aspect of mindfulness practice. Body scanning is often done in a comfortable and relaxed position, such as lying down or sitting, and can be guided by an instructor or done on your own with the help of a recording or an app.

By using the questionnaire shared in the link at the bottom of this chapter, my clients can start to identify their key indicators of stress and become more aware of their stress levels. With this awareness, they can take action to manage their stress and prevent it from becoming chronic and impacting their physical and mental health.

Imagine driving a car and suddenly hearing a strange noise. If you ignore the noise and continue driving, the problem could worsen and potentially lead to a breakdown or accident. However, if you immediately take notice of the noise and investigate the cause, you can fix the issue before it becomes more serious.

Similarly, when we experience symptoms of stress, it's important to create awareness and investigate the cause, rather than ignoring them and allowing the problem to worsen. By taking notice of our body and feelings, observing changes in our physicality and well-being, and identifying key indicators of stress, we can address the issue before it becomes chronic and has a more significant impact on our lives. Just as taking care of our car prevents breakdowns and accidents, taking care of our mental and physical health prevents burnout and other negative consequences of chronic stress.

Step 2: Impact

In the Powerful A.I.M.S Principle®, the second step is **IMPACT**. Once we have created awareness of our key indicators for stress, it's important to reflect on how our behaviour and relationships have been affected. Stress can have a negative impact on relationships, job performance, and physical health, so understanding how it impacts us is crucial to developing effective stress management strategies.

To establish the impact, we can start by reflecting on how stress affects our behaviour and relationships. It's important to recognise any behaviour changes and their impact on our surroundings, relationships, and work performance. We should also identify how stress has impacted our work performance, relationships, and physical health.

It's also important to consider any incongruences between our behaviour and values. Do we feel congruent with how we are behaving? If not, what changes can we make to align our behaviour with our values?

If we refer back to Sammie, you will recall, that she described herself as an individual experiencing challenging situations, that she went from 0 to Defcon 9, in 60 seconds, and subsequently shoot from the hip, become frustrated and react in a negative and impulsive way, that could potentially impact her relationships, professionally and personally.

By understanding the impact it was having on herself and those around her. It helped her to realise that she needed to keep her "Emotional Monkey" in check, and take a moment to reset and refocus. Which meant Sammie was able to take a more measured approach with her response to a situation. Which created a win-win situation for everyone.

This is a great example as to why we should also consider how our behaviour may be impacting others and the surrounding environment. This can help us identify areas where we need to improve and make positive changes.

Finally, researching evidence to support the impact of stress on behaviour and relationships can also be helpful in gaining a better understanding of how stress affects us and those around us. By understanding the impact of stress, we can develop effective strategies to manage it and improve our overall well-being.

Step 3: Motive

Establishing the **MOTIVE** behind your stress is crucial in finding the root cause of your key indicators and identifying strategies to make positive change. This involves questioning why you are experiencing stress and what the underlying reasons may be.

External factors can influence the motive, such as the people, places, events, and circumstances in your life. By asking questions such as when, where, who, what, and how, you can start to identify specific triggers that lead to stress.

However, the motive can also be influenced by past experiences in our lives, our beliefs, and values. These past experiences can shape our thoughts, emotions, and behaviours and ultimately impact our stress levels. It is important to examine these past experiences and beliefs to better understand how they are contributing to your stress.

By understanding your motives for stress, you can start to build a picture of what is causing your stress and how it is impacting your life. This awareness can help you to identify specific strategies and actions that you can take to manage your stress more effectively. It can also help you to identify any beliefs or patterns that are no longer serving you and may need to be changed in order to reduce your stress levels.

Our motives and beliefs can have a significant impact on our personal and professional lives. They can often limit us and prevent us from reaching our full potential, growing, and becoming fulfilled and successful. This is because our beliefs and motives shape our thoughts, actions, and decisions and can create unnecessary fears and doubts that hold us back.

For example, if you believe that you are not good enough to achieve a certain goal or succeed in a particular career, this belief can limit your efforts and prevent you from pursuing opportunities that could be beneficial to you. Similarly, if you have a fear of failure or rejection, you may avoid taking risks or putting yourself out there, which can also prevent you from growing and achieving your goals.

These limiting beliefs and fears can impact our confidence, self-esteem, and overall sense of fulfilment and happiness. They can also impact our relationships with others, as we may struggle with assertiveness or setting boundaries due to fears of rejection or failure.

Therefore, it is important to identify and challenge any limiting beliefs or fears that may be holding us back. This can involve exploring our motives and beliefs, examining where they come from, and questioning whether they are helpful or hindering our growth and success.

By doing so, we can begin to shift our mindset, increase our confidence, and pursue opportunities that align with our goals and values. This can lead to greater fulfilment and success in our personal and professional lives.

Step 4: Solutions

In this final step of the Powerful A.I.M.S Principle® - **SOLUTIONS** – it is important to find effective solutions for managing stress, and identify potential ways to reduce the impact of stress, prevent key indicators from occurring, or change behaviour patterns.

One example of a solution is exercise, which has been known to reduce stress and improve mental health. Another solution is relaxation techniques, such as meditation, deep breathing, or yoga, which can help reduce muscle tension and promote relaxation. Seeking social support from friends, family, or a coach can also be an effective way to manage stress.

In addition, setting boundaries and avoiding stressful situations can prevent key indicators of stress from occurring. This may involve delegating tasks or saying no to certain obligations to reduce workload and stress. It can also mean establishing new behaviour patterns, such as implementing new coping strategies or seeking professional help.

The Powerful A.I.M.S Principle® could be that of a gardener tending to their garden. Just as a gardener carefully selects and implements different strategies to keep their plants healthy and thriving, we too can carefully select and implement different stress management solutions to keep ourselves healthy and thriving. By identifying the root cause of stress and the impact it has on our behaviour and relationships, we can cultivate effective solutions to promote our personal and professional growth.

Sammie's experience with being vulnerable serves as a great example of a positive solution to managing stress. Initially, Sammie used to keep her challenges and struggles to herself, pretending to be a strong and stoic person. However, this led to her feeling overwhelmed, internalising her problems, and negatively impacting her health. Moreover, this behaviour also compromised her relationships, as she was not allowing others to support her.

When Sammie started to be vulnerable to those around her, it had a positive impact on her relationships, creating an environment of trust and openness. It enabled others to help her when they didn't know how to before, resulting in improved relationships, better performance, and reduced workload for Sammie. She was also able to get better sleep, which was no longer being disrupted.

Being vulnerable and reaching out for support can be a great solution to managing stress. It allows others to help and support you, which can lead to improved relationships, better performance, and reduced stress levels. By being vulnerable, you are showing strength and courage, and it can have a positive impact not only on your life but also on the lives of those around you.

In conclusion, the Powerful A.I.M.S Principle® is introduced as a framework for managing stress. Step 1 of the framework is creating **awareness** of the key indicators of stress and understanding how stress affects our mental and physical health. Mindfulness techniques such as meditation, deep breathing, and body scanning can help increase awareness of our internal state. Step 2 is reflecting on how stress **impacts** our behavior and relationships. It's important to identify any incongruences between our behavior and values and consider how our behavior may be impacting others. Step 3 involves understanding the **motive** behind our stress and identifying the root cause of our key indicators. Our beliefs and past experiences can shape our thoughts, emotions, and behaviors and contribute to stress levels. Finally, Step 4 is finding effective **solutions** for managing stress, which can involve exercise, relaxation techniques, seeking social support, and setting boundaries. Being vulnerable and reaching out for support can also be a positive solution to managing stress. By following the Powerful A.I.M.S Principle®, individuals can cultivate effective stress management strategies and promote personal and professional growth.

CHAPTER 10: THE PATHWAY TO PEACE: SORTING PATTERNS FOR SUSTAINABLE STRESS SOLUTION

"Happiness is not something ready-made. It comes from your own actions."

Dalai Lama

In this chapter, we will focus on the 3rd step of the Stress-Free R.I.S.K Resolution®, where we **SORT** an individual's patterns of behaviour between their key drivers and key indicators for stress, and develop sustainable solutions for managing stress. It is important to note that the patterns between the key drivers and key indicators for stress are different from the patterns established for each of these factors mentioned in isolation above.

We will also introduce the Pathway to Peace framework® in the next chapter, which can help individuals SORT their patterns of behaviour between their key drivers and key indicators for stress and develop sustainable solutions for managing stress. By doing so, individuals can create a foundation for long-term stress management and improved well-being.

The Wheel of (Mis)Fortune shown in diagram 3 is a tool that helps to illustrate these patterns of behaviour and their impact on our needs. We are creatures of habit and comfort, and it's easy to fall back into old patterns of behaviour. To avoid falling back into old habits, we need to take steps to reprogramme and retrain ourselves. This takes work, but the benefits will be significant on a personal and professional level.

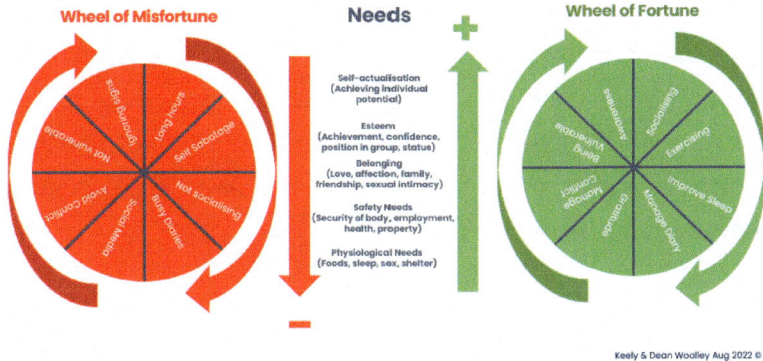

Wheel of Misfortune | **Needs** | **Wheel of Fortune**

Self-actualisation (Achieving individual potential)

Esteem (Achievement, confidence, position in group, status)

Belonging (Love, affection, family, friendship, sexual intimacy)

Safety Needs (Security of body, employment, health, property)

Physiological Needs (Foods, sleep, sex, shelter)

Keely & Dean Woolley Aug 2022 ©

Diagram 3 – Wheel of (Mis)Fortune

Some people believe that they can sustain change once they recognise their patterns of behaviour and simply implement new ways. However, this is not always the case. Accountability is key in sustaining change. When we have a coach or trainer to hold us accountable, we are more likely to keep up the momentum.

When we repeatedly engage in the "Wheel of Mis-Fortune" - working long hours, continuously scrolling on social media, self-sabotaging, sleeping poorly, avoiding exercise and conflict, not being vulnerable or socialising, and filling our calendars with endless business - we have a negative impact on our own needs in relation to Maslow's Hierarchy of Needs. However, if we reprogrammed these patterns to be more sustainable, we can create a "Wheel of Fortune" where our needs are positively impacted.

Retraining our beliefs and patterns can take work. However, the benefits of doing so can be significant, both personally and professionally, improving health, well-being, and performance. As Dumbledore once said, "sometimes there comes a time in life when we have to do what is right, even if it's not easy." By taking the necessary steps to retrain our patterns of behaviour, we can create a Wheel of Fortune, where our needs are positively impacted and we can sustain long-term stress management.

Joe Dispenza, is a well-known expert in the field of neuroscience and human potential, and his work highlights the challenges of rewiring our brains and changing our habits, particularly as we age. According to Dispenza, by the age of 35, our personalities and behaviours have become deeply ingrained and habitual, making it more difficult to change our ways.

This is where reprogramming our patterns of behaviour comes into play. By recognising the negative patterns that contribute to our stress, burnout, and imposter syndrome, and making conscious efforts to replace those patterns with more positive, sustainable ones, we can begin to rewire our brains and change our personalities.

However, as I mentioned previously, change can take work, and it requires consistent effort and dedication. We are creatures of habit, and it can be challenging to break free from our established patterns of behaviour. But the benefits of doing so can be significant, both personally and professionally.

By taking a mindful and intentional approach to reprogramming our habits and behaviours, we can create lasting change that positively impacts our well-being and overall quality of life. And with the support of mindfulness techniques, such as body scanning and other meditation practices, we can cultivate the self-awareness and self-love needed to make these changes and sustain them over time.

In conclusion, sorting an individual's patterns of behaviour between their key drivers and key indicators for stress, helps us to develop sustainable solutions for managing stress, and we can achieve this through the Pathway to Peace framework, which we will explore in the chapter

The Wheel of (Mis)Fortune illustrated in Diagram 3 demonstrated how our patterns of behaviour can impact our needs in relation to Maslow's Hierarchy of Needs. By reprogramming these patterns to be more sustainable, we can create a "Wheel of Fortune" where our needs are positively impacted, leading to improved well-being and performance.

Reprogramming our beliefs and patterns takes work and dedication. It requires consistent effort and accountability to sustain change. However, the benefits of doing so can be significant, both personally and professionally.

As we age, our personalities and behaviours become deeply ingrained and habitual, making it more challenging to change our ways. But with the support of mindfulness techniques, such as body scanning and other meditation practices, we can cultivate the self-awareness and self-love needed to make these changes and sustain them over time. By taking a mindful and intentional approach to reprogramming our habits and behaviours, we can create lasting change that positively impacts our well-being and overall quality of life.

CHAPTER 11: THE PSYCHOLOGY OF SECONDARY GAIN IN STRESS MANAGEMENT AND HOW IT INFLUENCES OUR PATTERNS OF BEHAVIOUR

"Change is hard because people overestimate the value of what they have and underestimate the value of what they may gain by giving that up."

James Belasco and Ralph Stayer

Stress is a common occurrence in our lives, and many of us try to alleviate it by making changes in our behaviour, lifestyle, or environment. However, what happens when we find ourselves stuck in a cycle of stress that we can't seem to break free from? Often, there is an underlying psychological reason that keeps us trapped in our stressful patterns, and one such reason is Secondary Gain.

Secondary Gain is a term used in psychology to describe the subconscious benefits that we receive from maintaining our current behaviour or situation, even if it is stressful or negative. In other words, we may not consciously want to be stressed, but on a deeper level, we may be gaining something from it.

For example, let's say you have a demanding job that is causing you a great deal of stress. You may consciously want to reduce your stress levels by finding a new job or changing your work environment. However, on a deeper level, you may be gaining a sense of identity, purpose, or accomplishment from your job. By leaving it or changing it, you may feel like you are losing a part of yourself, even if it is causing you stress.

This is where the Stress-Free R.I.S.K Resolution® framework can be useful. By identifying the key indicators of stress, as well as the patterns of behaviour that maintain them, we can begin to explore whether there are any underlying psychological reasons for our stress.

For example, if we find that we are constantly taking on more responsibility than we can handle, we may need to ask ourselves why we feel the need to do so. Is it because we want to feel needed or valued by others? Or is it because we are afraid of saying no and facing conflict or rejection?

Once we identify the potential secondary gains of our stressful behaviour, we can begin to challenge and reframe them. We can explore alternative ways to fulfil our needs or desires, without resorting to stress-inducing behaviour. We can also learn to tolerate discomfort and uncertainty, which may arise when we let go of our old patterns of behaviour.

The Stress-Free R.I.S.K Resolution® framework provides a holistic approach to stress management, one that recognises the interconnectedness of our physical, emotional, and psychological well-being. By integrating the concept of Secondary Gain into our understanding of stress, we can gain a deeper insight into our own patterns of behaviour and begin to create lasting change.

I have already mentioned that my client Sammie, was working over 70-hr weeks. Which was having a significant impact on her energy levels, focus and physical and mental health. Interestingly, it wasn't because she couldn't trust her team, didn't like delegating, or that she really needed to work those hours. Sammie, hadn't even taken a holiday in at least 2 years.

When I spoke about the secondary gain, during our group training session, and how people are often doing something, to avoid facing the real issue. There was a magical moment, when Sammie suddenly looked up, from taking notes. Her jaw dropped and you could see she had suddenly had a

Eureka moment. She realised, this was her, and this was why she had been working, such long hours. Sammie, was trying to avoid facing a personal issue, that she didn't want to face. Afraid, to say it out loud. If Sammie, didn't talk about it, then it might go away. The reality was, by not talking about it, then she was internalising the problem, it was eating away at her and it became even harder to face.

That very night, Sammie finally opened up about the personal issue and had an honest conversation about how she was feeling and thinking with her family. Sammie, also opened to her team the very next morning. In both cases the impact of being vulnerable, open and honest, created any environment where they all felt they could do the same. They shared some of their fears and concerns, and also thanked Sammie for allowing them to support her.

The benefit of this one Eureka moment, has helped Sammie to build an environment of openness and trust, in her relationships both personally and professionally. Sammie, no longer felt the need to work such long hours. Plus, Sammie finally took some personal time out for herself, and went on a proper date with her husband.

In conclusion, the Psychology of Secondary Gain highlights the importance of exploring the subconscious reasons for our stress, and how they may be maintaining our current patterns of behaviour. By using the Stress-Free R.I.S.K Resolution® framework, we can identify these underlying reasons and begin to challenge and reframe them, leading to a more sustainable and fulfilling way of living.

CHAPTER 12: THE POWER OF BECOMING CONSCIOUSLY AWARE OF OUR SUBCONSCIOUS

"The secret of change is to focus all of your energy, not on fighting the old, but on building the new."

Socrates

Becoming consciously aware of the subconscious mind is an essential aspect of managing stress and addressing limiting beliefs. Our subconscious mind is responsible for up to 95% of our thoughts, emotions, and behaviours, often without us even realising it. This means that if we want to make lasting changes in our lives, we need to address the root causes of our subconscious programming.

Many of us have limiting beliefs that hold us back from achieving our goals and living a fulfilling and successful life, personally and professionally. We often form these beliefs in childhood and can be deeply ingrained in our subconscious mind. For example, you may have grown up believing that you're not good enough, that you don't deserve success, or that you're not capable of achieving your dreams.

To manage stress and overcome these limiting beliefs, we need to become consciously aware of them and actively work to reprogram our subconscious mind. This involves identifying our negative thought patterns and replacing them with more positive, empowering beliefs.

One effective way to do this is through mindfulness techniques, such as meditation and body scanning, which allow us to tune into our subconscious mind and observe our thoughts and emotions without judgement. By becoming more aware of our subconscious programming, we can start to identify the limiting beliefs that are holding us back and work to replace them with more positive, empowering ones.

In addition to mindfulness techniques, it's also important to practise self-reflection and self-awareness. This involves taking the time to reflect on our thoughts and emotions, and how they may be contributing to our stress and limiting beliefs. By becoming more aware of our patterns of behaviour, we can start to make conscious choices to change them and create a more positive, fulfilling and successful life.

Overall, becoming consciously aware of the subconscious mind is crucial for managing stress and addressing limiting beliefs. By actively working to reprogramming our subconscious programming, we can overcome our negative thought patterns, reduce our stress levels, and achieve our full potential.

And consider this, according to Psychology Today, they have cited that we have over 50k thoughts per day, of which over 50% are negative thoughts, and ironically 90% are from the previous day. Imagine the results we can achieve, if we can transfer those negative thought patterns, into positive thoughts.

The idea of becoming consciously aware of the subconscious mind is a common concept in the field of psychology and personal development. It is often associated with the work of Carl Jung, Sigmund Freud, and other prominent psychologists. In terms of managing stress and limiting beliefs, the concept of conscious awareness of the subconscious mind is often used in various mindfulness and cognitive-behavioural therapies. It is also discussed in various books on personal growth and self-improvement, such as "The Power of Your Subconscious Mind" by Joseph

Murphy and "Breaking the Habit of Being Yourself" by Dr. Joe Dispenza.

In the next chapter, I will share how to establish patterns of behaviour between your key drivers and indicators for stress by following the 4 step process for a Pathway to Peace.

In conclusion, becoming consciously aware of the subconscious mind is essential for managing stress and addressing limiting beliefs. Our subconscious mind is responsible for the majority of our thoughts, emotions, and behaviours, and addressing the root causes of our subconscious programming is crucial for making lasting changes in our lives. By identifying negative thought patterns and replacing them with positive, empowering beliefs through mindfulness techniques and self-reflection, we can overcome our limiting beliefs, reduce stress, and achieve our full potential. The concept of conscious awareness of the subconscious mind is a common concept in the field of psychology and personal development, and is used in various therapies and self-improvement books.

CHAPTER 13: FINDING THE FOREST: THE FOUR STEPS TO LASTING WELL-BEING

"The more you know yourself, the more clarity there is. Self-knowledge has no end."

Jiddu Krishnamurti

Step 1: Clusters

The first step in the Pathway to Peace, is to **CLUSTER** our stressors based on who we were with, whether we are with family and friends, work colleagues, or strangers. The Clusters are groups of people that you may interact with regularly, semi-regularly or as strangers. It's important to identify these clusters because each group can have different dynamics and triggers that lead to stress or burnout. For example, the dynamics in a family and friend group can be different from a colleague group or stranger(s), and therefore, the stressors can be different as well.

It may, of course, be big groups of people that may have an impact. Whether they are known, or unknown.

I know, for instance, that both my husband and daughter really don't enjoy being in large groups, where the volume of conversation may be higher than normal, with multiple conversations going on around them. It doesn't matter that whether they are with family, friends or strangers, it still has a negative impact on them and their concentration, subsequently increasing their stress levels, creates anxiety and causes them to have headaches and brain-fog.

Step 2: Categories

We continue by breaking these clusters down into further categories, allowing for a more detailed understanding of the group and its dynamics. For example, within the family and friend cluster, you may have immediate family, extended family, close friends and acquaintances, etc... Within the professional cluster, you may have team members, peers, direct reports, senior leaders, suppliers, customers, etc.

Family and Friends:

- A family member who is aggressive or has a history of emotional abuse.

- A friend who constantly relies on you for emotional support without reciprocating.

- A family member who has different values or beliefs and is not accepting of your own.

- Feeling pressure to attend family gatherings or events that cause discomfort or anxiety.

- Professional:

- A senior leader who creates a toxic or hostile work environment.

- A poor culture or lack of communication within the workplace.

- A heavy workload or unrealistic deadlines.

- A team member who is uncooperative or difficult to work with.

Strangers:

- Fear of judgement or rejection from strangers.

- Feeling nervous or shy in social situations.

- Dealing with rude or aggressive strangers.

- Being in a crowded or unfamiliar environment.

These are just a few examples, but they illustrate how different factors within each category can contribute to stress levels.

It's worth noting that each of these types can provoke and trigger different emotions, patterns of behaviour and indicators.

Step 3: Classifications

Once you have identified these clusters and categories, it's important to classify them based on the problems they present. This could include identifying the emotions that they trigger, patterns of behaviour that arise, or specific reactions that occur. This step allows for a deeper understanding of the issues that may be causing stress or burnout in each group.

The analogy of not being able to see the wood from the trees is very relevant when it comes to managing stress. When we are caught up in the day-to-day stresses of our lives, it can be difficult to see the bigger picture and identify the underlying patterns of behaviour that contribute to our stress. We may feel overwhelmed and unable to make positive changes.

However, by taking a step back and looking at the situation as a whole, we can start to see the forest for the trees. We can identify the different clusters that contribute to our stress, such as family and friends, work, and personal beliefs. We can then break down these clusters into smaller categories and identify the specific triggers and patterns of behaviour that contribute to our stress.

Peeling back the layers of the onion in this way can be a powerful tool for managing stress. By gaining a deeper understanding of the different clusters and categories that contribute to our stress, we can develop targeted strategies for managing each one. We can also start to see how the different clusters and categories interact with each other, and how changes in one area may impact other areas.

Step 4: Criteria

The Pathway to Peace framework provides a four-step approach to managing stress and achieving lasting improvements in overall well-being. The final step is to establish clear **CRITERIA** for success. This involves identifying specific metrics or indicators that will be used to measure progress towards these goals. By doing so, individuals can more easily track their progress, identify areas where they need to focus their efforts, and celebrate their achievements along the way. This step is critical for ensuring that the changes made through the first three steps of the framework are sustainable.

It's important to break down stressors into manageable chunks and approach each situation with the appropriate level of attention and effort. The criteria for change is crucial in this regard as it allows for a manageable approach to addressing stress and burnout. Some situations may be more complex than others, and some may require more practice, so it's important to approach each one with the appropriate level of attention and effort.

The criteria for success may include reduced frequency and severity of stress-related symptoms, increased feelings of calm and relaxation, improved relationships with family, friends, and colleagues, greater success in achieving personal and professional goals, and enhanced physical health and well-being.

To make sustainable changes to reduce stress, it's important to create a personalised plan for managing stress, understand the level of stress and complexity of change required, and implement strategies that work best. By doing so, we can establish a clear pathway towards peace and well-being.

As the saying goes, it's often hard to see the forest for the trees. By establishing clear criteria for success, individuals can take a step back and see the beautiful forest of their progress towards lasting stress management and peace.

In this chapter, we learned about the first step in the Pathway to Peace framework, which is to cluster our stressors based on different groups of people we interact with regularly. By identifying these clusters and breaking them down into further categories, we gain a deeper understanding of the specific triggers and patterns of behaviour that contribute to our stress, then we can classify them based on the problems they present. This allows us to develop targeted strategies for managing each one and establish clear criteria for success.

We also learned that peeling back the layers of the onion can be a powerful tool for managing stress. By gaining a deeper understanding of the different clusters and categories that contribute to our stress, we can more easily track our progress, identify areas where we need to focus our efforts, and celebrate our achievements along the way.

The quote from Jiddu Krishnamurti emphasizes the importance of self-knowledge and how it can lead to greater clarity in managing stress. And by establishing a clear pathway towards peace and well-being, individuals can make sustainable changes to reduce stress and achieve lasting improvements in their overall well-being.

CHAPTER 14: THE PATH TO LASTING CHANGE: BUILDING A SUSTAINABLE STRESS MANAGEMENT PLAN

"Change is not a destination, it's a journey. You don't suddenly arrive at change one day; rather, it's a process that takes time and effort."

Dr. Samantha Boardman, clinical instructor in psychiatry and assistant attending psychiatrist at Weill Cornell Medical College

In the previous chapters, we have explored the key drivers and indicators of stress, established patterns of behaviour, identified examples of strategies and solutions for change by understanding ourselves on a deep-level and for responding to stressful situations. Now, it's time to put all of this knowledge into action by building a sustainable plan that will help you manage stress in the long-term.

The **KICKSTART** step within the Stress-Free R.I.S.K Resolution® is all about taking small, easy, and quick-win steps towards change while also incorporating longer-term sustainable solutions, as we established in the Pathway to Peace.

In this chapter, we will discuss how to build a sustainable plan to manage your stress, burnout, and imposter syndrome effectively. We will focus on small, easy, quick-win changes and longer-term changes that are sustainable and will help you achieve lasting results. Time management is an essential component of this plan, so we will discuss how to manage your time effectively to prioritise your self-care and manage your stress.

By incorporating small, easy, and sustainable changes into your life, you can build a plan that will help you manage stress in the long-term. Remember, change takes time, but with patience and perseverance, you can achieve a healthier, happier, and more fulfilling life.

In an article written in Forbes – Leadership Strategy – they quote Andrew Shatte, PhD, **meQuilibrium's** Chief Science Officer, says, "It's not the plight that determines your stress response. It's your ability to get up and see your way through it." We are wired to search for danger on the horizon, but the survivors are the ones who stay focused, optimistic and believe in their abilities—while taking measures to improve their own resilience.

Here are some examples of how we can KICKSTART the process, build momentum and implement sustainable change

Small, Easy, Quick-Win Changes:

- It's important to start with small, easy, quick-win changes to build momentum and increase confidence.

- Taking regular breaks throughout the workday, such as a short walk or stretching.

- Practice deep breathing exercises for a few minutes each day.

- Incorporate regular exercise, even if it's just a short walk or stretching routine.

- Write down three things you're grateful for each day.

- Taking a few minutes to disconnect from technology and engage in a mindful activity.

- There is a big emphasis on celebrating small wins to stay motivated. For example, you might treat yourself to a favourite snack or take a few moments to appreciate your progress.

Longer-Term Changes:

- It is important to recognise that you will need to make longer-term changes to address the root causes of stress, burnout, and imposter syndrome.

- Setting boundaries to protect your time and energy, such as establishing specific work hours and avoid communicating and checking emails after a certain time to prevent burnout.

- Delegating tasks & responsibilities to others or seeking support from others to reduce your workload to reduce overwhelm and manage your stress.

- Prioritize self-care activities, such as exercise, meditation, or spending time with loved ones.

- Seek support from a therapist or a coach to work through imposter syndrome.

- Build a support network of friends, family, or colleagues who can offer guidance and encouragement.

- Engage in personal development activities, such as reading, attending workshops, or taking courses.

- Ensure you create a plan to implement these changes gradually over time. This might involve setting specific goals and tracking your progress to stay motivated. And as mentioned in the Pathway to Peace, build a criteria for change and a measure for success.

Time Management for Self-Care:

- A key and important factor is managing your time effectively to prioritise self-care.

- Create a daily schedule or to-do list to stay organised and remain focused. Set priorities to ensure that self-care activities are included.

- Minimise distractions, such as turning off notifications and sounds on your phone or close your emails while working on a task. Particularly, during dedicated self-care time.

- Set aside dedicated time each day for self-care activities, such as meditation or exercise.

- Prioritise sleep and create a bedtime routine to ensure adequate rest.

- There is a huge emphasis on the importance of setting aside dedicated time for self-care activities, such as exercise, meditation, or hobbies. This might involve scheduling these activities into your daily or weekly routine. Booking them into your calendar, means you are more likely to take time out for yourself. If it is not in your diary, then every day work-life tends to take precedence.

Tracking Progress and Adjusting the Plan:

- It is important to track your progress and adjust your plan as needed.

- Use a journal or an app to log your self-care activities, stress levels, and mood. Are great tools to capture your progress over time.

- Regular reviews of your plan to ensure that it is still working for you and make adjustments as needed, helps to sustain improvements. This might involve checking in with yourself on a daily or weekly basis and making changes to your plan based on your progress and feedback.

- Celebrate small wins along the way to stay motivated.

- Seek feedback from others, such as a coach or accountability partner, to identify areas for improvement.

By incorporating small, easy, and sustainable changes into your life, you can build a plan that will help you manage stress in the long-term. Remember, change takes time, but with patience and perseverance, you can achieve a healthier, happier, and more fulfilling life.

Building a sustainable plan is like building a sturdy house. You need to start with a strong foundation and then add small, incremental changes over time to make it stronger and more resilient.

In the next chapter, I will introduce the Holistic Recuperation Recipe, which provides tips, tools, techniques and strategies that you can implement and sustain in your everyday life and achieve immediate sustainable results to prevent or reduce stress levels, learn self-care and self-love, and improve your overall wellbeing and mental & physical health.

In conclusion, building a sustainable plan to manage stress, burnout, and imposter syndrome is crucial for achieving long-term well-being. By incorporating small, easy, and sustainable changes into your life, you can build a plan that will help you manage stress in the long-term. It's important to start with small, easy, and quick-win changes to build momentum and increase confidence. And then, you need to make longer-term changes to address the root causes of stress, burnout, and imposter syndrome. Effective time management is also essential in prioritizing self-care and managing stress. It is important to track your progress and adjust your plan as needed, seeking feedback from others, and celebrating small wins along the way to stay motivated. Remember, change takes time, but with patience and perseverance, you can achieve a healthier, happier, and more fulfilling life.

CHAPTER 15 – "HOLISTIC RECUPERATION RECIPE – THE ULTIMATE HOLISTIC GUIDE TO WELL-BEING AND SUCCESS"

"In today's rush, we all think too much — seek too much — want too much — and forget about the joy of just being."

Eckhart Tolle

Step 1 - Stop

As we have established in previous chapters, when you start feeling overwhelmed, frustrated, angry or any other negative emotions, it's important to take a step back and literally stop what you're doing. This is because stress triggers the release of cortisol, which can increase your blood pressure, heart rate, and other physiological responses that can lead to chronic stress, anxiety, and depression. Taking a break, breathing deeply, and refocusing your attention on something else can help reduce the effects of stress on your body and mind.

Research has shown that taking breaks throughout the day can help improve cognitive performance, reduce stress levels and improve overall well-being. Additionally, studies have shown that deep breathing exercises can help reduce the levels of cortisol in your body and improve your body's stress response.

As mentioned, stopping and taking a break from the hustle and bustle of everyday life can have numerous benefits for our well-being, health, and performance. Some of these benefits include:

1. Reduced stress levels: When we stop and take a break, we give ourselves the opportunity to disconnect from the stressors of our daily lives. This can help to reduce our stress levels and provide a sense of calm and relaxation.

2. Improved physical health: Taking a break can also have physical health benefits, such as reduced blood pressure, improved digestion, and decreased muscle tension. It can also provide an opportunity to engage in physical activity or exercise, which can further improve physical health.

3. Improved mental health: Stopping and taking a break can provide an opportunity to prioritise our mental health by engaging in activities such as mindfulness, meditation, or therapy. This can help to improve our mood, reduce symptoms of anxiety or depression, and improve overall mental well-being.

4. Increased creativity and productivity: Taking a break can also help to boost our creativity and productivity by allowing our minds to rest and recharge. It can provide a fresh perspective on problems or challenges, leading to new and innovative solutions.

5. Improved relationships: Finally, taking a break can improve our relationships with others by providing the opportunity to connect with loved ones, spend quality time together, and engage in activities that promote social connection and support.

In summary, taking a break and stopping can have significant benefits for our overall well-being, health, and performance. It provides an opportunity to disconnect from stressors, prioritise our physical and mental health, boost creativity and productivity, and improve our relationships with others.

Step 2 - Switch-off

Technology and social media have become an integral part of our daily lives, and while they offer many benefits, they can also contribute to stress and anxiety. By setting aside time throughout the day to switch-off from technology, we can reduce our exposure to external stressors and create more space for mindfulness and relaxation.

Research has shown that excessive use of social media and technology is associated with increased stress levels, anxiety, and depression. By limiting your use of technology and social media, you can improve your focus, increase your productivity, and improve your overall well-being.

The biggest challenge I see, is that people often spend many hours using technology, even when it is not necessary.

I often hear from female executives, leaders, founders and entrepreneurs, "I am too busy"; "I don't have time"; "I don't have the opportunity for a break, or to meditate, go for a walk or exercise", or "I can't complete my endless list of tasks" etc.. and yet, when I ask how much time do you spend on social media, answering emails, watching YouTube, reading notifications or texting. I am often greeted with a small grin, and a slightly shamed face, when they reveal that they often spend far too much time on their phones, and can while away many hours on irrelevant distractions.

What's worse, they go on to tell me the first thing they reach for in the morning, and the last thing they put down, is their mobile phones. Neither of which has a positive impact on your cortisone levels. For the most part, it may stimulate anxiety and stress levels, because you are needing that instant gratification, when you post something on social media, and then waiting for someone to respond and likes your post, or you may read an article or post, that may cause you frustration or anger. Alternatively, it may be emails you are receiving from work colleagues, suppliers on customers, expecting an immediate response and you feel you must reply.

This will also have an impact on your relationships, as you are spending more time looking at your phone, rather than engaging with the key people in your life.

When I worked with my client Maisie Stanyon, this was one of the key things that she said she was guilty of, as was her partner. And yet, when she made a conscious effort to reduce the amount of time on her phone, she felt immediate improvements with her stress levels.

Maisie switched off her sound and notifications on social media, emails and messaging, to prevent her from being distracted. Maisie even created different folders on her phone, so she would only access the areas specifically associated with business. E.g. banking, accounting systems and business systems. Plus, Maisie implemented some rules, e.g. not touching her phone in the morning, other than to turn off her alarm, until she was at work. And when she got home in the evenings, she and her partner put their mobile phones to the side, and made sure they didn't touch their phones during dinner, or whilst watching a programme together.

And finally, not touching their mobile phones when they went to bed at night.

These changes not only had a positive impact on her availability of time, it improved their relationship, their sleep and reduced her stress and anxiety levels.

According to a 2021 report by Statista, the average time spent on mobile devices in the United States is around 234 minutes per day, or approximately 3.9 hours. This includes time spent on social media, messaging apps, browsing the internet, and using other mobile apps. However, the amount of time spent on technology can vary widely depending on the individual's age, occupation, and lifestyle. Some people may spend significantly more or less time on their devices, depending on their personal habits and preferences.

According to a study by Nielsen, adults between the ages of 35-49 spend an average of 6 hours and 58 minutes per week on social media, while adults between the ages of 50-64 spend an average of 4 hours and 9 minutes per week on social media. However, it's worth noting that this study did not specifically measure the time spent on other technology-related activities, such as reading/responding to texts and notifications, watching YouTube, TikTok, etc.

Imagine how much time we could free up to focus on our own self-care and self-love.

"We're losing connection with the things that matter most, like our relationships, our health, and our sense of purpose. The good news is that we have the power to reclaim our lives by being more

mindful and intentional about our use of technology." Christina Crook

Step 3 - Sustenance

When we neglect the importance of the third step of the Holistic Recuperation Recipe - Sustenance, we put our mental and physical health at risk. Poor eating and drinking habits can have numerous negative and chronic effects on our health, ultimately leading to decreased performance and increased stress levels.

For instance, consuming unhealthy food and drinks can lead to obesity, heart disease, weakened immune system, bone and muscle damage, low energy levels, disrupted sleep patterns, impaired brain function, hypertension, stroke, heart attack, and increased risk of cancer.

However, when we make a conscious effort to improve our nutrition, we reap significant benefits that improve our performance and reduce our stress levels. By implementing changes in our diet, we can improve our sleep quality, enhance brain function and cognitive abilities, increase physical health and energy levels, and ultimately improve our overall well-being.

Eating a healthy and balanced diet can significantly impact our physical and mental health, leading to improved productivity and overall life satisfaction. Therefore, it's essential to prioritise the sustenance aspect of the Holistic Recuperation Recipe to achieve optimal health and performance.

"Let food be thy medicine and medicine be thy food." Greek physician Hippocrates, known as the father of modern medicine

A great quote, which emphasises the importance of good sustenance in promoting health and well-being. Just as medicine can heal the body, so can the right food and drink nourish it and help it thrive.

Step 4 - Sleep

The final, yet key step in the entire Holistic Recuperation Recipe, is SLEEP. In fact, according to Matthew Walker, a sleep expert and author of the book "Why We Sleep," sleep is one of the most undervalued and important things we should prioritise for our health and well-being.

"Sleep is the Swiss army knife of health. When sleep is deficient, there is sickness and disease. And when sleep is abundant, there is vitality and health." Matthew Walker

Sleep is essential for our physical and mental health, and lack of sleep can have a significant impact on our overall well-being. Chronic sleep deprivation can lead to increased stress levels, weight gain, decreased immune function, and a host of other negative health effects.

Research has shown that getting enough high-quality sleep can improve cognitive function, reduce inflammation, and improve overall well-being. Additionally, practicing good sleep hygiene, such as avoiding electronics before bedtime and establishing a regular sleep schedule, can help improve sleep quality and reduce stress levels.

Here are a few key tips to contribute to a good night's sleep:

- Being consistent with the times you go to bed and get up every day helps to improve your circadian rythmn/sleep patterns

- Exposure to sunlight first thing for at least 20 seconds every morning helps to train your body's inner "sleep clock". Circadian rhythm. The sunlight helps your body make a brain chemical called serotine that plays an important role in your well-being

- Darkness is key to a good night's sleep, which is why it is important to remove and switch off technology in your bedroom. Matthew Walker, recommends that you dim your lights in the house, and hour before you go to bed and it helps you to develop a sleepy feeling

- Ensuring your bedroom is around 18.5° c or 65° f will help to improve sleep. When you are too hot, you become restless and have discomfort, because you become dehydrated or sweaty, which means sleep becomes challenging

- Switch off technology at least an hour before bed. Don't use in your bedroom, as the blue light – stimulates the brain, boosts alertness and can make it harder to fall asleep. Which suppressing the production of melatonin, the hormone that helps regulates the sleep-wake cycle

As you know, Sammi has had many Eureka moments in relation to her management of stress. The topic of SLEEP, was a huge wake up call for her. Now Sammi had this habit of thinking that the reason she was awake late at night was that this was when her creative juices were flowing.

When, in fact, what it actually meant was that her brain wasn't shutting down. Her cortisone levels had gone through the roof, where she was so stressed and when she really looked at what she considered creativity, was not at all. As during the day, Sammi needed to rethink what she had been working on late at night, or what took her several hours at night. She would have achieved in half the time during the day, because Sammie wasn't so tired and wired.

But when Sammi had found time to stop, switch-off and her sustenance improved, it meant that she did start sleeping properly. Her brain was not racing or creating noise.

And during the day, her focus had improved, along with her ideas and creativity. Plus, she took time out to discuss her ideas with her partner and colleagues, which made them feel engaged in her decision-making and idea generation.

Overall, the Holistic Recuperation Recipe framework is designed to help individuals reduce stress levels and improve their overall well-being by taking a holistic approach to health and wellness. By implementing these four key steps, individuals can create a foundation for a healthy and balanced life, both personally and professionally.

Conclusion: By implementing the strategies in this chapter, you can build a sustainable plan to manage your stress, burnout, and imposter syndrome. Remember to start small, celebrate your wins, and prioritise your self-care by managing your time effectively. By tracking your progress and adjusting your plan as needed, you can achieve lasting results and maintain a sense of balance and well-being in your life.

CHAPTER 16 - "THE G.E.M.S WELL-BEING JOURNEY®: PRACTICAL STRATEGIES FOR RE-ENERGISING AND OVERCOMING BURNOUT"

"Take care of your body. It's the only place you have to live."

Jim Rohn

This chapter is a provides an insight to into my holistic recuperation pillar from my "Freedom Transformation Formula®", which emphasises the importance of managing stress to achieve optimal well-being. It provides you with actionable steps to reduce stress levels and prevent burnout.

In my next book, I will expand on this pillar by introducing The G.E.M.S Well-Being Journey®, which focuses on re-energising and injecting vitality into one's life through gratitude, exercise, meditation, and sleep. My new book will complement this current book by providing you with additional tools and strategies to support your overall recuperation process.

However, I wanted to share these additional actionable steps which you can implement to complement your sustainable plan and begin your journey to a stress-free, fulfilling and successful life:

1. Mindfulness: Incorporating mindfulness practices into your daily life can have a significant impact on reducing stress and improving overall well-being. Mindfulness involves being present in the moment and fully engaged in what you are doing, without judgment. It can involve practices such as meditation, yoga, or simply taking a few deep breaths and focusing on the present moment. By practicing mindfulness regularly, you can train your mind to be more resilient to stress, improve your ability to focus, and enhance your overall sense of well-being.

2. Self-Care: Self-care is essential for managing stress and preventing burnout. It involves taking time for yourself to engage in activities that bring you joy and promote relaxation. Self-care can take many forms, such as taking a hot bath, going for a walk in nature, or simply reading a book. It's important to make self-care a priority and schedule it into your day to ensure that you are taking care of your own needs.

3. Boundaries: Setting boundaries and learning to say no is an important aspect of managing stress and preventing burnout. It involves understanding your own limits and being able to communicate them effectively to others. This can involve setting boundaries around work hours, saying no to additional responsibilities when you are already feeling overwhelmed, or simply taking a break when you need it. By setting and respecting your own boundaries, you can reduce the risk of burnout and protect your own well-being.

4. Healthy Habits: Developing and maintaining healthy habits is another important strategy for managing stress and preventing burnout. This can involve engaging in regular physical activity, such as exercise or yoga, eating a healthy and balanced diet, and getting enough restful sleep. By taking care of your physical health, you can improve your ability to manage stress and increase your overall sense of well-being.

5. Support Systems: Building and nurturing support systems is critical for managing stress and preventing burnout. This can involve reaching out to friends and family for emotional support, seeking professional help from a coach, trainer or therapist, or joining a support group for individuals who are experiencing similar challenges. I will share a link to my Free Facebook Group, Female Executives, Leaders & Entrepreneurs: BounceBack from Burnout-out at the end of this chapter, where you can join other individuals in a supportive community. By building a support network, you can increase your resilience to stress and feel more connected to others, which can have a positive impact on your overall well-being.

Remember, it's important to find the strategies and techniques that work best for you and incorporate them into your daily routine. By making a commitment to prioritise your well-being and taking action to manage stress and prevent burnout, you can achieve greater success and fulfilment in your personal and professional life.

CHAPTER 17: CONCLUSION - THE POWER OF INTEGRATING HOLISTIC WELL-BEING STRATEGIES FOR LONG-TERM SUCCESS

"Cultivate the power of self-awareness and transform your beliefs & patterns of behaviour. The journey may be challenging, but the rewards of well-being and success are worth the effort."

Keely Woolley

In this final chapter, we will bring together all the key concepts and strategies discussed throughout the book and explore how they can be integrated into a comprehensive approach to managing stress and achieving long-term well-being.

We have learned about the link between our beliefs and burnout, as well as the key drivers and indicators of stress that impact our daily lives. We have explored techniques for responding rather than reacting to stress and managing our emotions effectively, breaking free from people-pleasing and understanding the connections between our patterns of behavior and stress. We have also delved into the power of becoming consciously aware of our subconscious and the psychology of secondary gain in stress management.

By following the Relaxing Road M.A.P.S® system, we have identified and sorted our patterns of behavior for sustainable stress solutions, building a personalized stress management plan that takes into account all aspects of our well-being. We have also explored the holistic recuperation recipe and practical strategies for re-energizing and overcoming burnout, such as mindfulness, nutrition, exercise, and sleep.

I have shared the next pillar in my "Freedom Transformation Formula®" in relation to **RE-ENERGISE** - The G.E.M.S Well-being Journey® which provides a practical framework for integrating holistic well-being strategies into our daily lives, incorporating the principles of gratitude, exercise, mindfulness, and self-care. By embracing this approach and adopting a growth mindset, we can overcome obstacles and achieve our full potential, both personally and professionally.

In conclusion, by integrating the concepts and strategies presented throughout this book into a comprehensive well-being approach, we can achieve long-term success and fulfilment. By prioritising our well-being and taking a holistic approach to managing stress, we can unlock our full potential and lead fulfilling, happy, and healthy lives. The power lies within us to take control of our well-being journey and achieve our goals, and this book provides the tools, guidance, and inspiration to do so.

To learn more about how you can become a private client or enrol in the next Stress-Free R.I.S.K Resolution® -12 week programme – scan the QR Code below to book a call.

Metamorforsuccess
Click on the QR Code for a Free "Discovery Call"

LinkedIn Profile: https://urlgeni.us/linkedin/BBBO

Instagram Profile: https://www.instagram.com/metamorforsuccess/

Facebook Business Page: https://urlgeni.us/facebook/FLBB

Mobile Phone: 07458195786

OBJECTIONS

In writing this book, I recognise that some readers may have objections or doubts about the strategies and ideas presented here. I want to take a moment to address some of these concerns and offer my perspective.

Objection 1: I don't have time to implement these strategies.

I understand that many of us have busy schedules and feel stretched thin. However, I firmly believe that taking the time to address your stress levels is crucial for your long-term success and well-being. The strategies outlined in this book are designed to be practical and efficient, and I encourage you to carve out even just a few minutes each day to focus on stress reduction.

Objection 2: These strategies won't work for me.

Everyone's journey is unique, and what works for one person may not work for another. However, I believe that the strategies outlined in this book have the potential to benefit anyone struggling with stress and its effects. It may take some experimentation and tweaking to find what works best for you, but I encourage you to approach this process with an open mind and a willingness to try new things.

Objection 3: I'm sceptical of self-help books in general.

I understand that the self-help genre can sometimes be viewed with scepticism. However, I believe this book is different; it is rooted in research and evidence-based practices, and the strategies presented here have been shown to be effective in reducing stress and improving overall well-being. I encourage you to approach this book with an open mind and a willingness to engage with the material.

By addressing potential objections head-on, I hope to alleviate any concerns or doubts readers may have and encourage them to fully engage with the strategies presented in this book.

Printed in Great Britain
by Amazon